The Cat

(n) The cute little boss who rules your house with an iron paw.

This edition published by Ravette Publishing 2019.

Ravette Publishing Limited
PO Box 876, Horsham, West Sussex RH12 9GH
info@ravettepub.co.uk
www.ravette.co.uk

ISBN: 978-1-84161-411-3

Best Friend

(n) The cat.

RAVETTE PUBLISHING

Cattitude

(n) What you get when you don't feed kitty on time.

Personal Space

(n) Something the cat is unaware of.

Cat

(n) A strange creature which would as soon gouge your eyes out as it would cuddle you.

URBAN WORDS

Pawrenoia

(n) A fear that your cat is up to something (they are).

Cat

(n) A fluffy alarm clock.

Plants

(n) Little pieces of nature that you are not allowed to have.

House

(n) A building owned and operated solely for the comfort and convenience of the cat.

URBAN WORDS

Cute

(n) Just how the cat looks – shortly before clawing your face off.

Cat

(n) Something you think is cute but is obviously plotting your demise.

URBAN
WORDS

Meow

(n) A loud noise the cat makes – usually at 3am!

Lives

(n) Something the cat is running short of.

Table

(n) A device used to hold items for the cat to knock off with a paw.

Cat Food

(n) What you buy in bulk just as the cat decides he doesn't like it anymore.

URBAN WORDS

Furmiliar

(n) When the cat wraps itself around your legs.

Money

(n) It can buy a lot of things but it can't curl up on your chest and purr when you've had a rough day.

URBAN WORDS

Kitten

(n) A homicidal muffin on legs.

Cat

(n) The only member of your family you actually like.

Indifference

(n) A facial expression perfected by the cat.

URBAN
WORDS

Furburbia

(n) Your living room when the cat is shedding fur.

Catholic

(n) A person addicted to cats.

Midnight

(n) The time of day that the cat decides to run randomly from one side of the house to the other.

URBAN WORDS

Gift

(n) A dead creature. With love from the cat.

Litter

(n) An absorbent substance that the cat likes to spread everywhere in the house.

URBAN WORDS

Death
Stare

(n) That look
the cat gives
you regularly.

Cat Mum

(n) Someone who works hard so her cats can have a good life and always has room for one more.

URBAN WORDS

Feline Paralysis

(n) The condition in which a person is unable to move due to the presence of a cat on their lap.

Cats

(n) Children
with fur.

Pawprint

(n) An indelible mark cats leave on your heart.

Home

(n) Wherever my cat is.